Purple Rays

Of Sunlight

VALLI KUMAR

Purple Rays of Sunlight

© 2020 Valli Kumar

Cover artwork by Prabath. Image of Valli Kumar is self-portrait captured by the author herself.

First Print December 2020

ISBN: 978-1-0879-2574-5

Published by Valli Kumar

Acknowledgments

Behind every successful mom, there is an army of tiny tots and a devoted husband who can make it happen and crown her with that deserving title of which she can be proud. My story has been no different. Writing has always been my passion and writing a book that is so close to my heart wouldn't have been possible without the support of my husband, Prem, and my two boys, Rohan and Rian. My younger one would sometimes critique my work and even make suggestions that I ended up using in my book, and reminded me that one is never too young to offer suggestions and one is never too old to accept those wholeheartedly. My older one referred me a book cover designer whom he knew and his referral worked out really well. I am immensely pleased with the thought that both my boys played an integral part in shaping my book and were excited to contribute to it becoming a reality.

I would like to thank my parents for their constant never-ending support and encouragement. I know my mom is extremely proud of me and that thought makes my heart full with happiness and contentment.

I would like to thank Shannon Babcock, for proofreading my book in a short span of time, I sincerely appreciate her effort and time. The book cover designer translated my idea into a reality beyond my expectations to convey my purpose through his cover design, special thanks to Prabath. I also take this opportunity to thank many others who helped with the publishing of my book.

Last but not least, I would like to thank the prospective readers of my book for purchasing their copy, hoping to get a good read. I promise I have put in my best efforts to provide one, and you will not be disappointed.

Table of Contents

Preface

How it all Began –

When I told my kids I was going to write a book, my younger one responded quite baffled, "Why would you want to write a book? Don't you have to be famous to write one?!" That cracked us all up, and all you could hear was the resonating laughter at the dining table, which by the way probably may have perked up our neighbors, giving them the notion that their friendly neighbors had just gone crazy. It is good to laugh out loud now and then, even if the joke is on you. Laughter is a special ingredient to a healthy heart. After our healthy heart conversation, I told them that if an ordinary person like me has successfully managed to juggle life (which as of late has been pretty intense) and has been able to carve out a niche of personal happiness for myself and create a positive impact on others who surround me; and if one, just one, other person can take inspiration from my writing and create their own bubble of happiness, my purpose will have been realized.

Chapter 1 - Cradle Bliss

Back to the beginning…almost 45 years ago, a little angel dropped a blessing into my mother's womb, and whether it was a boon or a bane to society, that blessing was the birth of me. My mere existence in this world created happiness for the people around me. My parents were happy, my grandparents were happy, my neighbors were happy, and people I knew and those I didn't know were happy. Back in those days in India, around the 1970s, milk was brought to our home by the milk man, and newspapers were thrown every morning by the newspaper man. They would say to my mom, "Heard you had a baby after a long time? God bless the girl baby." Basically, the entire street knew the day I was born and started kicking life. My life was celebrated. I was being celebrated without even my knowledge, creating ripples of happiness to those around me. Why not resonate that happiness to those around me now? Point noted. I will come back to this later. I promise.

Birth of life creates happiness to those around,
Little does the Newborn know,
That her birth would bring a smile to those that
surround.

I definitely do not remember all of my formative years, though I vaguely remember a couple and distinctly remember a few. I was not a child who threw tantrums. Now that's a blessing for a parent! Maybe it was one of those things I definitely do not remember. But I do vaguely remember, or I should say I distinctly remember, that I was a tad bit naughty as a child. Nevertheless, my parents loved me, put me on a high pedestal and fed me with a silver spoon. Don't get me wrong, my parents were strict, but my degree of naughtiness didn't cause or inflict injury to second parties. It was all self-inflicted, causing me a few broken bones now and then. My house had a huge verandah with two benches, around three feet off from the ground, the idea being that a guest can comfortably sit with his or her legs not dangling in the air but firmly placed on the ground. For a two- year-old that was a perfect hopping place, and I would jump from one bench across another…no surprise about the broken bones. I must have experienced some degree of pain, but I do not remember it. What was constant in all those micro incidents was the smile on my face. I realize why that smile never faded away in those years. It was because I felt secure, wanted and cared for, and I mirrored those exact feelings to those around me. Feeling happiness within and spreading happiness without, comfortably creating my own bubble of happiness.

Her little heart knows no fear
For Love is all she treasures
No shackles to confine her happiness
For happiness has no bounds of measure
Magic is all she sees
For love is the language she speaks.

Me, Year: 1978,
Place: Chennai, India

    Every parent adores their child, regardless of whatsoever (beady eyes, pinto nose, with eyebrows, without eyebrows, with dimples, without dimples). Children mean the world to parents. Daughters will always be daddy's little princess and boys will always be a mother's fine young prince. It was no different for me. I was my dad's princess. I vividly remember how my dad furnished a truck load of sand to be placed on the outward side of the benches in the verandah, just to avoid more broken-bone episodes. Trucks are called Lorries in India. Though they not as huge as Americanized "trucks", they are quite large and a lorry full of sand warrants notice! My dad would have brought me the moon on a stick had I wanted a moon lollipop. I am sure many of us have similar treasured memories subconsciously etched on our minds that we can recollect decades later and still feel the emotions gushing through.

It is funny to note that as we grow up, our human brain desires to selectively remember certain events and forget those that we wish to forget (selective amnesia), which runs counter to the fact that an adult brain, being much larger in size than a younger brain, can recall more. Studies show that young infant brains can recall both implicit memories and explicit memories, though not as much as an adult brain can. Implicit memory is the unconscious learning that is exhibited in a child right from his or her infant days. Examples are the ability to recognize familiar faces and objects and to display emotions accordingly, or the happiness expressed by a baby on seeing his or her mother bring a familiar milk bottle during feeding time. The reason, as explained by experts, is that those parts of the brain that are responsible for this encoding, processing, retention, and retrieval are the striatum, the cerebellum, and the amygdala, which are believed to be the first to mature and be fully developed in an infant, in their first postnatal months [1]. Whereas, the explicit memory of a child reaches maturity around the age of eight to ten months. Children from as young as two years old can recall episodic memories of events scattered throughout their early lives [2]. It involves the ability to piece together individual details around an incident to recollect at a later date. This involves portions of the brain, particularly the temporal lobes of the hippocampus that plays an important role in memory retrieval, and is believed to attain almost full maturity to that of an adult sans the finer details [3], which is likely one of the reasons why toddlers are able to recall certain events that are close to their hearts.

I am not a neuroscience expert, nor a medical doctor, nor a psychologist, trained to provide indications of how human memory relates to child development or explain how a child can recall his or her episodic memory. What I can vouch for is my own personal experience. My attempt to sprinkle some intense information about brain/neuroanatomy is to provide a basic understanding for the reason behind my ability to recollect some wonderful memories from the past.

A certain famous Sparkling Tooth toothpaste from the 1980s! I am sure a lot of folks remember it from back then. I do not remember the taste or brushing with it, but I remember it came with small wonders within the box! Yes, the box is all I remember, for it held precious tiny toys that a three-year-old longed to hold. When I think about it now, I presume there were no choking hazard lawsuits back then. Maybe there were, but I never swallowed any. However, on a separate occasion, I have stuffed a small eraser up my nostril during those formative years. That's a whole different story. I had to be taken to the doctor's office to get the eraser removed. Now I know why the pediatrician of my kids jokingly said to one of them on their annual checkup, "Let me check if you have any Crayons up your nose…" That triggered parts of my brain to recall the infamous event of the not-so-famous mom. The toys were extremely small, around the size of a penny or even smaller, wonderfully made with some sort of plastic material, and included a range of animals and marine life to satisfy the appetite of a three-year-old. I remember playing with the toys by hiding them in the sand box and then digging through piles of sand to retrieve them. That is the kind of memory recall I am talking about. We all have similar stories to tell from our childhood that we cherish forever. As the story goes, when I was little (still in the toddler years), apparently I was in the habit of throwing things around, like plates, cups, and spoons. I would not heed to anyone asking me to stop throwing things onto the ground. One fine day, tired of repeated attempts to get me to stop, my mother had said to me, "If you keep throwing things around, you will not have anything to give to your children." That was it! That was all it took for me to stop throwing stuff around. Maybe that was why I saved the plastic eraser toys that I collected when I was a young toddler to give to my future children. I recently handed them over to the Gen Alpha in my family. Transcendence of happiness from Gen X to Gen Alpha.

Chapter 2 - Got to be Loving Life at First Sight

It is widely known that children weaning out of toddlerhood look for companionship outside of their immediate family circle. A child's bubble of happiness is expanded further to include friends, neighbors, teachers, and many more around. According to my perception, about this time, friends make up seventy percent of a child's life. Friendships help children develop social skills, and they learn to communicate with one another and gain self-confidence and self-esteem. They learn to navigate the wild waters, resolve conflicts on their own, and negotiate a solution that works for all. Through that process, they learn to respect one another and care for one another. During this time, friends mean the world to them, and there is no better place to make friends than at school.

I can vividly recall my first day at school where I happily waved goodbye to my mom and sprinted away, ready to make new friends. Back in those days, everything was rustic and organic. We sat as a class and had lunch underneath huge mango trees. Darn those crow droppings that would fall right into our lunch boxes, we never minded those anyway…we would scoop them out and eat the rest. I know, it's ghastly, and probably a reprise of a similar incident now would demand a different course of action. But back then it provided hours of giggles for my friends and me, and we would excitedly wait to see who the next victim was going to be. All that mattered to the young mind was having fun and being happy irrespective of the situation. It was time well spent exploring childhood.

Walk with me my friend,
For I will not leave you behind,
Walk with me my friend,
For I will lend my shoulder for you to cry,
Walk with me my friend,
Together our strides will make us stronger,
All set to conquer what may come before us,
To wherever our little strides may take us.

Late October to early November in the southern part of India, namely in Chennai, the city where I am from, is usually bombarded with back-to-back hurricanes. It is the monsoon season setting in. Children tend to develop a distinct affinity for water play and love the earthy smell of rain, commonly referred to as the petrichor. I remember being glued to the news channel on the television, praying that schools would not be shut down due to excessive flooding. The norm was that the schools would be closed if the classrooms flooded. On days that we did have school on rainy days, I would brim with joy at the happy thought of making paper boats and racing them with my friends. Splish, splash, and splosh, I would be drenched in muddy water from head to toe, but would return home with the biggest grin on my face. The problem of washing muddy white shirts to sparkling whiteness was not mine, though lo and behold my mom groaned and moaned while at it. To the benefit of many, there were some suggestions provided by the television commercials on how to turn brown shirts to spotless white shirts.

Hopefully that alleviated some painful heartaches of working mothers. Nevertheless, I was living life to the fullest. That was the way it was meant to be. It was loving life at first sight and never looking back. Happiness knew no bounds and measures, no boundaries or rules to confine one within. I tend to harp on the subject of happiness as somehow as I grew up, it was lost in translation during the transition to adulthood. Conscious efforts were made to retrieve it.

Love from grandparents is always a double delight to a child, as they rarely utter the word "no". Grandparents are an integral part of a child's blossoming years and provide unconditional love and care. A memorable part of my childhood was spending time with my paternal grandparents in their city, a trip that was kick-started with the excitement of an overnight train journey. We played with indigenous materials, and seeds from plants were utilized as moving coins in games. A very rustic game board, Mancala, also known as the Pallanguzhi in my regional language, furnished endless hours of fun and joy. Seeds from the tree, Kalyana Murungai, generated heat when rubbed against the floor, and had the property of retaining heat for up to a few seconds. We used these as moving coins. We used to rub the seeds to see whose felt hotter to touch! This served as perfect revenge when one was playing with peers. I revamped this beauty during my last visit to India and with a little touch of new paint, it is back to its glorious state.

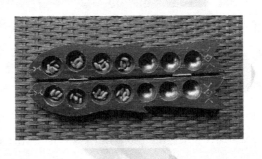

Mancala (Pallanguzhi)

Just as I was finishing elementary school, we moved to the United States where I completed middle school and part of junior high. My mother's friend from the 1970s in College Station, Texas,

24

embraced me as her Indian granddaughter and showered me with love and affection. Schooling was indeed different in many ways, in stark comparison to schooling back in India, but adaptation was not an issue. Making friends was relatively easy back then. All I had to do was follow a cat in our apartment complex and that tailgate eventually lead to its rightful owner. Voila! And so, very quickly, my bubble of happiness expanded to include other people from all walks of life. By all means, life was not perfect nor rosy all the time for a ten-year-old, and there were occasional meltdowns; but it was all about focusing on the positives and just being happy. Children are not perfect little people and do not exhibit such expectations. Maybe that reason of not having to be perfect all the time was the reason for my inner happiness and harmony.

Every child considers himself or herself to be in a happy place in life at around this time. Security, food, and material benefits are provided for, and they therefore spend their time and energy exploring other activities and figuring out what works for them. My friend Blue painted the town red and so did I. My friend Green went for dancing classes and so did I. Green played volleyball. So did I. Orange played basketball. So (wanted) I. Yellow decided she wanted to learn a new language. So (wanted) I. Black and White decided to give karate a try. So (wanted) I. The "wants" outnumbered the "dids" and that was perfectly acceptable. Eventually I figured out what worked for me and I ended up playing volleyball for the school all through my school years. Basketball was just a reason to hang out with my best friend, and eventually they figured out that I was no good at it and kicked me off of the team. Language classes were not up my alley either, and the main attractions were the snacks the teacher provided after the class was done and the fact that we could play with her kittens. Don't kids love food prepared by other moms! So did I.

Chapter 3 – Battle of the Dreams

Let's skip ahead a few more years and halt at high school. This was no doubt the toughest phase in my life. Even if I had to look back at forty-something years, I would still pick my high school years to be the most challenging chapter. By this time, we had returned to India and I was ready to face my adolescence and teenage years with the same enthusiasm and zest. Hormonal changes, psychological changes, and emotional changes, coupled with peer pressure to excel in whatever I laid my hands on, was more than what a young adult could handle.

Perfectionism or fear of failure can lead to an immense buildup of anxiety and depression. For eons, generations after generations, the stance is the same irrespective of the advancement in every field of study. My mother has gone through it all. I can definitely vouch that I certainly did, and I can see my children being right in the midst of it now. Most young adults do not acknowledge that they need help or a support system to pull through their adolescent struggles. Fortunately, or unfortunately (for some), the type of environment provided to them largely influences their ability to handle these challenges. Parents, counselors, pediatricians, all play an important role in recognizing the child's struggles and helping them manage their emotions and alleviate their misery. Friends are still important at this stage and one is lucky if they find that support system to lean on. Parents often feel they lack the right chord to connect with their child, and often underestimate their efforts to do so. Every attempt is worthwhile. Parents need to engage in deeper conversations with their teenagers in order to evaluate the ability of the young individual to convey what is going on and discover ways to overcome it [4].

Who am I?
What has become of me, I do not know,
Where is me, my identity, I forage through,
Changes in my body I certainly decry,
The reason for my emotional barrage I can tell,

Meanwhile, my mind rustles through the cloudy
haze,

Trying to comprehend it all at once,

My mind says one,

Though my heart says another,

A bustle of thoughts race through my mind,

Sinking deeper into the abyss every time,

*Looking for that **purple ray of sunlight,***

To guide my wandering path,

Where do I fit in, I ponder,

Silent whispers speak to my mind and heart,

Affirming I do not need to fit in,

I can be me, for there is no one else like me.

Parents take pride in every little thing that a child does no matter what and never lose an opportunity to plaudit them. If a child could catch a fly with his or her tongue, what an immense sense of pride would kick in about how talented the child was in trapping a fly, and the talent would immediately be displayed on a pedestal. Every visitor would have to bear the endurance of witnessing the talent, much to the embarrassment of the kid and sometimes the visitor himself. Despite the predicament of talent on national display, everyone loves a pat on the back. Children feel accomplished and gain a sense of self-confidence. Low self-esteem, feelings of worthlessness, depression, and insomnia often are bearings of impassive involvement of the concerned.

Sometimes, the pride a parent takes in displaying the accomplishments can stretch quite too far, or just a tad bit. Everyone has a family member or a friend who would be more interested in you "becoming" something than your parents themselves, or you yourself for that matter. Well, I had one too. A certain visitor, an uncle (in India, any gentleman about the age of the father is regarded as an uncle), would spend about ten to fifteen minutes bragging about how his children Tom, Duck, and Harry secured such high grades that they were offered understated seats for the so-called three lifelines of Doctor, Engineer, and Lawyer. A pause after that would only provoke the question of which of the three I wanted to become. I sometimes wished the uncle would have selective dementia and forget I even existed! On one such occasion of random visits paid by the uncle, I mustered enough courage to respond "none of those". It wasn't that I was a rebellious kid. It was more about giving me the freedom to explore more options. By all means, these three mainstream fields of education are the greatest choices and provide financial stability and security, but life as I saw it was much larger than the platter of options in front of me.

It was the battle of dreams, or rather the lack thereof.

More so, nightmares! It was the nightmare of not "becoming" one of these, and what if I failed in life because I didn't make the magical choice that Tom, Duck, and Harry did. I was afraid to speak out, ashamed at not knowing what I wanted to "become", and not being ready to declare it to the open world. So the next time the uncle would come home, I would have an answer. It was during this time, my mother coaxed me into reading the Positive Thinking books which really helped me overcome my 'dis'-ability to address my becoming. It is great if one knows in high school exactly what they want to do and strives toward it. I was one of those who didn't have a career choice back then. According to me, I can place juniors and seniors into three categories: a large percentage who know exactly what they want to do, a smaller percentage who know what their parents want them to do, and a certain percentage of kids who don't have a concrete idea of what they want to do. According to a survey, an estimated twenty to fifty percent of students enter college undecided, and an estimated seventy-five percent of students change their majors at least once before graduation [5]. There was no time to squander thinking about what was next, I was going with the flow and next thing I knew I had already embarked on something. That something may not have been the career pathway that I would have desired to find myself thirty or forty years from then, but nevertheless I had something to hold onto. I had secured state first in the Architecture Aptitude Examination, and therefore the natural pathway was to study Architecture for my undergrad studies. Soon after, I realized that maybe it wasn't meant for me, but there was no going back. I had similar flashbacks through my five years of the architecture program which I managed to shut behind doors. I was not as bright as the sun, nor as sluggish as the sloth, but I made sure I was the best worker bee ever. I put my heart and soul into whatever I did and made sure I put my best foot forward and didn't retract back. Meanwhile I had already formulated my plans for my post-graduate program in the United States and I worked hard toward that. I discerned that the society and those that surrounded me didn't break me. They in fact molded me to what I have become today. I realized that it is perfectly fine if I didn't know what I wanted to become when I was sixteen years old. Life provides you with opportunities at twenty-four, thirty-six, and any time you desire to make that change; what mattered was that I worked hard at sixteen, twenty-four, and thirty-six. I am a senior IT professional now at one of the largest consulting companies in the world, and I have found my happy place. I take pride in what I do today and I love my job. I mentor those who once were like me on the other side of the unknown land, and who wished to sail across. It is a matter of choice. There is no expiration date on when and what to achieve something or become successful. However, there is no excuse for being impassive, lethargic, or for showing a lack of zest in whatever we do.

Chapter 4 – Self Realization

Once we have successfully managed to etch out our individual pathways in becoming what we have desired to become, we have by then succeeded in fulfilling the most basic necessities in life. Abraham Maslow describes the next phase as self-attainment as it pertains to human developmental psychology in his 1943 paper "A Theory of Human Motivation" in *Psychological Review* through the five-tier hierarchical pyramid of needs.

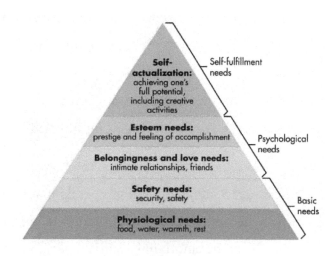

Image referenced from Maslow's Hierarchical Needs by Saul McLeod, Updated March 20, 2020 [7]

Factors that lead to stage five, self-realization, mandate that stages one through four are satisfied. First and foremost, in stage one, our physiological needs are met. Well, they are sort of met. Humans can stretch this need pretty far, and this need keeps getting larger and bigger until they reach a point at which they begin to downsize again. When an individual joins with another and becomes two, the search begins for a decent-sized home. And when the household becomes four, the search expands for a bigger house, and we aren't content with that. Vacation homes! Wouldn't we all love to own that perfect vacation home by the river in the woods…with a mountain view. Well, Maslow isn't addressing those excessive wants now. He is addressing the basic needs getting fulfilled.

Having fulfilled tier one, the human mind then seeks to safeguard and protect its interests and being. The need for a sense of security and safety arises. It can be emotional security, personal safety, or protecting the interests described at the tier one level. Tier one and tier two go hand-in-hand and make up the basic necessities of every human being.

Once the basic necessities have been furnished, people look to establish social relationships beyond their family members. Social and societal skills tend to be the dominating factor in determining and establishing meaningful relationships. People look to earn self-respect and positive acknowledgment from those with whom they interact (within the relationships established in the previous tier). They feel compelled to satisfy their personal accomplishment, dignity, and self-esteem. It is all about giving the self a pat on the back. This can also lead to self-exploration for other sources of self-recognition, thereby leading to discovery or newfound passions for other activities, such as hobbies. A few years ago, I discovered my passion for painting and art. During a recent trip to Iceland, we witnessed the magnificent aurora borealis, also known as the Northern Lights. It created a profound impact on my mind, and I decided that upon our return I wanted to recreate that magic in the form of an acrylic fluid painting. Not only did I thoroughly enjoy creating a piece of art that I would be proud of, but I proudly hung it for display. It is only human to seek recognition for something into which you have put your heart and soul.

Dancing into the darkness of the Northern Skies,

Unfurling my magnificent iridescent veil as I go,

Some say my mystical appearance brings good fortune,

Wherefore brings forth my alluring and mesmerizing celestial glow,

For I am the goddess of the dawn, I am Aurora.

Self-actualization or self-realization is the
need for an individual to feel accomplished, realize
his or her full potential, and keep pushing his or her
ability to perform better and better. Self-realization,
by definition in the Western understanding, is the
"fulfillment by oneself of the possibilities of one's
character or personality" (see also self-actualization,
Merriam Webster dictionary). I perceive this as a
growing experience, learning to self-realize what
potential we have to unleash in every phase of life.
Life throws different scenarios, actors, and settings
at us all the time to spice it up. As we all know,
change is the only constant in life. And with every

new learning experience, we walk away with a self-realization thought or retrospect on an aspect that our human mind had not been exposed prior. I do not believe I would regard this as self -attainment during this early phase of my life. To me, it is mostly value-driven, a self-discovery process in every walk of life, which motivates me to be the best version of myself in whatever endeavor I take on. It is the exercise of having complete control of emotions, mind over action, a grip over fear, stress, and anxiety. This doesn't happen overnight, especially in the early phases of one's independent stature. I myself remember hours of crying behind closed closet doors trying to reason out why my best efforts at times were not rewarded or recognized. It is a constant effort of oneself to overturn the negative experiences and create a positive course of action, getter better at it every time. Through that process, we begin to eliminate the distractions around us and focus on the positives, turning that into a positive force. It does by no means equate to perfection; simply put, it is the striving of oneself towards achieving contentment for one's efforts.

Fables and fairytales are short stories intended to convey very powerful messages to young readers, and we have all enjoyed reading them at some point in time. The golden moral values they convey hold true even as we age. Sometimes, once in a while, a reminder of one of those reinforces our convictions and helps us regain our confidence and self-worth. I would like to narrate an abridged version of a simple fable that we all read in our younger years: *The Ugly Duckling* by Hans Christian Andersen.

As the story goes, a mother duck raises a raft of ducklings and finds one duckling to be larger and uglier than the rest. The "Ugly" duckling's siblings bullied her and secluded her from their fun and frolic. The ugly duckling felt miserable and lonely and wanted to run away. And so she did, until she embarked upon a rock, near a pond, which she decided she would make her home. The Mallard ducks that swam in the pond called her ugly too and asked her to leave. She was rejected and tormented wherever she went. She gathered courage to fly across several hundred miles until she came upon a cottage. There too she was scorned for her appearance and shunned away from the rest. The winter season had ended, little did she know that she had turned into a beautiful and graceful swan. Spring had returned and she saw a group of swans in the pond and she longed to be among them. Soon, the other swans acknowledged her and invited her to be part of their raft. She was quite bewildered and only then she saw her own reflection in the pond and realized her self-worth and was no longer influenced by negativity around her, for she was born to shine. The moral of the story is that there are always negative influences around us that may cause us to feel dejected and depressed and instigate a feeling of worthlessness, but they are temporary, and when those feeling do arise, we should make attempts to rise above it all and not succumb to it easily.

Chapter 5 – Gray Defines Me

As an individual gains confidence and realizes his or her potential and self-worth, there arises a sense of individualism. We no longer feel compelled to fit in, but we desire to stand apart. We tend to formulate our own value systems and beliefs and abide by them. We no longer feel the need to please everyone for our own individual choices. It by no means indicates that we turn rebellious against society; we still need to abide by the moral, social, and economic rules of society. But what I would like to convey is that having a personal belief or a value system that addresses the ideals that a person embraces in making personal choices is no longer influenced by what the society directs or forces them to do. It takes a lot of courage to stand apart from the crowd and be noticed, recognized, and respected. Eventually, we are known for the decisions we make and the values we believe in. In that process, I learnt to create my own identity and a place in society that uniquely defines me.

Soon we realize that life is not all about being one hundred percent right or wrong, there is no definite black or white demarcated answer to all, and it is perspective that marks the presence of one or the other. Categorical falls within the Shades of Gray in a color spectrum.

Gray defines who I am. I realized that Gray looks good on me.

A few years ago, a certain dress, a blue-and-gold striped dress, scorched the internet. We have all succumbed to one of those color blindness exercises wherein we would excitedly see which color spectrum each one of us observed. Each person's brain would comprehend and interpret the color differently; it was blue and black or white and gold. Some even saw it as pink and brown and some as gray. In fact, it turned so notably viral that there has been a dedicated Wikipedia page since, just for the famous dress [6]. The conversation can get deeper than the superficial color combination that people perceive, but for my purpose of an analogy, the point I am trying to convey is that there is no right or a wrong answer. As perception varies, so do the outcomes. Consider the play of light and darkness, it is widely understood that darkness is the absence of visible light—its polar opposite. Once again, establishment of the presence of light or darkness depends on the perspective of the viewer.

Light, absence of darkness

Peace, absence of internal chaos

Happiness, absence of fathoms

Yet, the omnipresence of both

Makes us appreciate the former.

Chapter 6 – Formidable Dominance

What defines us doesn't happen overnight.
Over a period of time, we begin to realize that
certain characteristics and our beliefs converge to
define who we are and help create our individuality.

Never settle for the Pixie Dust,

Reach for the golden stars,

For a star is just another star,

But each shines with all its might,

To mark its place in the Milky Way,

Shine brighter to create your own destiny,

Be you, and your individuality will shine

through.

Life throws curveballs at us all the time, and
we manage to dodge some and we get hit by some.
But when we do get hit, we manage to get up, dust
ourselves off, and join right back in the game. Our
beliefs and the value systems we uphold help us
navigate through these situations and assist to guide

us along the way. We often feel pressured to please everyone in the process and end up pleasing none.

I would like to narrate a small story to add some flavor, an Aesop fable to be precise. Aesop's fables are great. There is a moral to each story that reminds us constantly of things that we might forget. This story reinforces the concept that when we try to please everyone else around us, sometimes we end up pleasing none, and it can lead to some grave situations.

A miller and his son decided to sell their donkey in the market. On their way, they met a group of passersby who mocked them, saying that they were foolish to be walking alongside the donkey while one of them should be riding it. Hence, the miller decided to have his son ride the donkey. A few minutes after entering a village, another group of bystanders ridiculed them, indicating that it should be the father riding the donkey and not the son, since the son was very young and could endure the long walk to the market. Heeding the bystanders, the father hopped on the donkey and off they set to the market. Further along on their journey, a smaller group of travelers informed them that they would not be able to sell the donkey, as the donkey would have become weary and exhausted from carrying the father to the market. Immediately the father got off the donkey, the father and son duo tied the donkey to a pole, and they then decided to carry the donkey on their shoulders. This only led to more mockery, as some folks laughed so hard at the sight of them that it frightened the poor donkey, who kicked himself loose, fell over the bridge into the river beneath, and drowned. The miller and his son returned home bearing a huge loss due to having tried to please everyone.

The constant pushback from society and the pressure to fit in becomes intense at times, and we need to consciously make an effort to remind ourselves of who we are and what we believe in during those times in order to not lose our identity. It does not mean that we should be offensive to others in that process or turn a deaf ear to what others say; it simply means that we sometimes need to politely agree to disagree. This by no means implies that we lose our adaptability in the course of doing so. Adaptability is a good thing, and it enables us to progress and evolve. It has been one of the hardest of life's lessons for me, not to lose hope, not to lose my identity, and not to give in when my convictions and value system are compromised. There have been situations in which I have felt the loss of people close to my heart in doing so, but if the alternative meant that I had to lose my individuality and my belief of what was right, it did not warrant the attention it received. Otherwise I would end up like that zebra who doesn't know if he is black with white stripes or white with black stripes!

Advice is something that no one likes to hear. Eventually, we learn that not all advice is bad or detrimental to us, or directed with the motive to degrade us. Lending an ear to advice may teach us to view situations with a different eye. The degree of criticism that one can endure varies and negative criticism especially can hurt our self-esteem sometimes. But, it can in fact help us grow into better human beings if we can filter out those that will benefit us from those that would be deleterious to us. In other words, advice should be carefully taken with a pinch of salt.

Chapter 7 – Acceptance and Reconciliation

I learnt it the hard way that it is not about being the best in everything we do, but it's about delivering the best we can in all that we do. Life can sometimes be brutal and harsh, for which sometimes we are prepared, at other times the lessons we have learnt in the past help us prepare to overcome it, and at other times, we are entirely unprepared. Each and every time we face an impediment we become stronger—our inner being, our values, our discipline, and our beliefs help us emerge from the situation even stronger. I consider life to be a collection of experiences and the more varied they are, the more captivating it is. The collection is unfortunately not one that we can pick and choose, but the surprise packages do offer some zest to an otherwise mundane platter.

Our inner strength and our core beliefs make us the person we are, and our acceptance of who we are defines us and our place in society. We accept our strengths, our weakness, and our values, recognize their impact on those around us, and the repercussions and reconciliations along the way. We realize very quickly that we face certain hardships in our journey, namely the desire to be "liked" by everyone. Everyone yearns to be liked by everyone else, in real, in reel, or on social media. Though I may approach the individual and the situation with the same compassion, passion and respect, I may not witness the same vibe I intend to in all circumstances. Some like me for who I am and some don't like me, for the same reason of who I am. This is perfectly acceptable to me, as human sentiments are not robotic. Those who share similar vibes to those of mine will empathize with me for the person I am. But accepting this reality does take time, a lot of courage, and a positive mindset to overcome disappointment and rejection.

My heart desires to be accepted for who I am,
For the pure intentions I behold,
Behind the curtain wall, there is no other me,
Me and myself as pure as it can be,

Set free from the shackles of falsehood,

True to self and true to thy,

Let my heart soar to fill its desire,

Compassion, passion, respect is all I offer,

My heart's content with happiness in return,

Inner peace and tranquility is all I see,

For there is no race to be liked,

I connect with those who share my vibe,

I respect those that feel otherwise.

Live my life as it can be,

True to me and True to thee.

We have all been through phases where there were moments wherein one felt the desire to be liked by everyone around. During my formative years, at the young age of six or seven years, I took a different approach to having people like me. I would ask my mother to buy me fancy erasers that came inside plastic toys and generously distribute them to my friends, grinning with happiness and the assumption that they liked me. After a week, the second round would start and my mother began to ponder at how much of writing a young toddler could do that was enough to exhaust about fifteen of those erasers. Even though the underlying fact is that sharing is caring, it is not the same when sharing is exchanged for bribery! Decades rolled by and this time around, I had given twenty dollars to my younger one for his school book fair. He brought home just a robotic eraser with no change in return, and then I was made aware that he bought sixteen of them to distribute to his friends on the school bus. Chuckling with laughter, I realized that, that indeed was the circle of life.

As adults, we have all succumbed to social media likes and hearts at one point in time or another. At this juncture, I would like to affirm the fact that I do sincerely appreciate all the comments, likes and hearts that are on my social media posts; and I do respond to each and every person that took the extra time from their daily life or routine to dedicate a like, heart, or comment on my post. But, as we all know, life is much larger than the likes and hearts. Sometimes, as much as it brings joy and happiness, it does bring its fair share of disappointment and sadness. Emotions play an important role in sketching the mindset of an individual and influences his or her behavior. It does take time and effort to overcome the urge and the desire to be liked and approved by everyone we know.

Self-worth, self-acceptance and self-realization accentuate the inner self, create an identity, and help mark our presence in this world; thereby creating the unique 'You'. The Purple Ray of Sunlight that we are scouring to help shepherd us in our journey is not around us, it is lit within us; all we need is that realization and reassurance to seek it from within.

References

(1) *Nelson, C. A. (1995). The ontogeny of human memory: A cognitive neuroscience perspective.* Developmental Psychology, *31, 723–738. doi:10.1002/9780470753507.ch10*

(2) *Richmond, Jenny; Nelson, Charles A. (2007). "Accounting for change in declarative memory: A cognitive neuroscience perspective". Developmental Review. 27 (3): 349–373. doi:10.1016/j.dr.2007.04.002. PMC 2094108. PMID 18 769510.*

(3) *Red Smucker-Green (Jan 1, 2017). When Do Children Start Making Long-Term Memories? SCIENTIFIC AMERICAN, a Division of Springer Nature America, Inc.*

(4) *Adolescence and Emotion, (July 19th, 2019) Carl E Pickhardt Ph.D.*

(5) *https://studybreaks.com/college/undecided-how-to-pick-college-major/ By Lexi Lieberman, University of Pennsylvania*

(6) *"The blue and black (or white and gold) dress: Actual color, brand, and price details revealed". The Independent. 27 February 2015. Archived from the original on 13 July 2019. Retrieved 10 May 2015.*

(7) *Website : Maslow's Hierarchy of Needs by Saul McLeod, March 20, 2020*

CPSIA information can be obtained
at www.ICGtesting.com
Printed in the USA
LVHW082016211220
674832LV00038B/929

9 781087 925745